The
KEY

The

KEY

GOD'S

SUPERNATURAL POWER'S

LINDA LINDSAY

Order this book online at www.trafford.com
or email orders@trafford.com

Most Trafford titles are also available at major online book retailers.

Scripture quotations marked KJV are from the Holy Bible, King James Version
(Authorized Version). First published in 1611. Quoted from the KJV Classic
Reference Bible, Copyright © 1983 by The Zondervan Corporation.

Print information available on the last page.

ISBN: 978-1-4907-6341-5 (sc)
ISBN: 978-1-4907-6347-7 (e)

Trafford rev. 08/10/2015

 www.trafford.com

North America & international
toll-free: 1 888 232 4444 (USA & Canada)
fax: 812 355 4082

Summary: This book is a true story of spiritual encounters in my life, shared testimonies of supernatural experiences. This included a chapter on Spirituality vs. Religion and the conversations developed in the spirit with Angels relating various assignments, being empowered by God to fulfill the work for Jesus in the supernatural. I speak about God's Supernatural Powers and how it affects our daily life and activities.

The Boeing Company Environmental toxic tort cases how God used documents that I had to reveal a cover-up, many people suffered from various cancers including myself which God did a miraculous healing. Many lives were lost including infants, children's, adults, some entire families watch to effects of their love ones suffer greatly. The company did nothing to rectify the loss of all the innocent blood that was shed. This was displeasing to God the Holy Spirit grieve for the cries of the people, because the company was not moved wickedness in high places. The Supernatural encounter when the Angel intervenes;

> *For we wrestle not against flesh and blood, but against principalities, against powers, against the rulers of the darkness of this world, against spiritual wickedness in high places. Ephesians 6:12*

When my name was changed to Grace by the Supernatural Power's of God this was the spiritual name that was given to me. How his wonderful works has brought me out of darkness into his marvelous light.

Scriptures quotations are taken from the King James Version.

To my mother
Loving memories
My brothers and Sister
For always being there

Contents

Foreword

But ye are a chosen generation, a royal priesthood, an Holy Nation, a peculiar people; that ye should shew forth the praises of him who hath called you out of darkness into his marvelous light. 1 Peter 2:9

Preface

Giving honor to Our Lord Jesus Christ who has given me the words by his Holy Spirit to help others to understand the Supernatural Power's and supremacy to operate in his power.

The purpose of the book is pertaining to the Supernatural Power's of the Almighty God. I was positive about sharing this information being inspired by the Spirit of the Living God, extremely concerned how the people of God can be encouraged through my testimony. Most will get the information that I have shared with fellow Christians over 30 years of my life; now God has instructed me to write the words in a series of books. Anyone who believes in the Holy Spirit can receive the same Supernatural Power's that Jesus has given to me for so many years. I know that we have to be trustworthy for God to open the ways of the Supernatural Spirit, there is a conscientiousness that comes with the power. If we're not being accountable to God he would have no hesitation to withdraw his Supernatural Power from his people and leave us powerless. We also have to be vigilant not to misuse his power, all power belongs to God. In this world today with the economy in a downfall, having the power from the Living God increases our capability and wiliness for a higher level of success in our endeavors. Not to compromise the Holy Spirit on our Christian walk, just to get their name in highlights of titles or money; or even being powerful. Good health absolutely not being sick again not even the flu virus, this all can be accomplished through the Supernatural Power of Jesus

Christ. We are all of the same Spirit that has accepted their calling and willing to work the assignment that God has given.

> *But ye are not in the flesh, but in the Spirit, if so be that the Spirit of God dwell in you. Now if any men have not the Spirit of Christ, he is none of his. Romans 8:9*

I have dedicated my life as a servant of Jesus Christ mostly being a soul winner for Christ; also a prayer warrior. Hoping to lead them to better life of knowing Jesus and watching lives being transform for the Glory of God, allowing Jesus to direct my path and reach hurting people, placing their needs in my heart basically doing God's will to his expectation. I believe the Holy Spirit has inspired me to write this book about his Supernatural Power's. The Spirit of the Living God came to me with the challenge saying "Now is the time to write the book" I was ready to do whatsoever God wanted from my life experiences. My prayer that the book would transform lives to make this world a better place to live, from generations to generations to come; the Lord has prepared me for this assignment.

> *God is a Spirit; and they that worship him must worship him in spirit and in truth.4:24*

Jesus is the door; Our Heavenly Father always has a plan and purpose, the enemy has no power over the "Blood of Jesus" I have learned to reach the empowerment of the Supernatural through obedience as a result of following the instructions of the Lord Jesus Christ reallocating to the next level. You do not use testimonies of the saints in the church to gain a profit in the world, and don't steal others testimonies as your own. My story is true and every word can be verified, Jesus has given me the power as an overcomer.

> *Fear none of those things which thou shat suffer; behold, the devil shall cast some of you into prison, that ye may be tried; and shall have tribulations ten days; "be thou faithful unto death, and I will give thee a crown of life. Revelation 2:10*

I believe that is why he changed my name to; "GRACE" it's because despite of all that I had endured I can still Love everybody only because of the Love that Jesus has given me. The most unbelievable message that I had ever encountered it left me with a lot of questions regarding my name changed by God; I couldn't shake it for nothing, once the name was dropped in my spirit I did struggle with it for over a week. Subsequently, I was attending Bible College in Seattle when I eventually start telling everyone about my name being changed by God; of course they were not ready to receive that message because all they did was give me this strange look without a word spoken. Then I decided to ask the instructor about when God changes your name, does that mean I would have to go to court and have it changed legally, or is it a change in the Spirit only. Apparently he did not have an answer for me and he took the question to the pastor, I never did get a response from anyone that's when I knew the message was authentic it came from the spirit of the living God Almighty.

When the Spirit of the living God said "I Have Change Your Name, and you will be called GRACE", I was in shocked for days and couldn't understand why God would change my name to the meaning of divine Love and Protection by the favor of God. Consequently, I was very uncomfortable with this message from God; I need to know why I was chosen to receive this calling, so I went searching for answers in the bible. I spoke about it in Bible College, speaking to many Pastors and Missionaries, finding no help just strange looks. Then I went to the Lord Jesus Christ and he made it plain I had reached a higher level in the spirit. Being more thankful and appreciative of what was given to me by God's divinity. Now the fruit of the spirit has a different meaning than what I was taught, this was found in the scriptures.

> *He that overcometh, "the same shall be clothed in white raiment; and I will not "blot out his name out of the book of life, but "I will confess his name before my Father, and before his angels. Revelation 2:5*

Having the ability to overcome hardship for Jesus Christ is a privilege and honor, while keeping your integrity and conducting your behavior so that the Love of God is portrayed thru the Holy Spirit. In this life we all have complication that compels us to react to our damaging approach, but as people of God we need to exercise a more positive attitude moving in the direction of Holy Spirit our comforter. Furthermore, taking the necessary steps to please the Lord Jesus and not being a manservant, only then will God trust you, with his ultimate level of Supernatural Powers.

Acknowledgments

I would like to thank the Pastor and Evangelist at International Full Gospel in California, who so warmly took a young woman and taught her the word of God. For the hours of late night studying and shared knowledge of ministering the word of God. Having the patient to proceed in Love until the foundation was completed.

Next I would like to thank the Pastor, and Evangelist at the Paradise Church of God In Christ/COGIC California, who was the motivation for me to appreciate every Praise and Worship.

Thanks to the State of Washington Jurisdiction of Church of God in Christ, where I served as an usher for several years with the organization.

Thanks to Christian Faith Center, Everett Washington for their ministry of Healing reaching a wounded servant of God.

Spiritual Warfare

When I found myself in the wilderness alone it was cold and dark, at times I was very lonely thinking Jesus was not with me, but he said "I will never leave, nor forsake you" he was there all the time. I knew it was spiritual warfare; it was time to get suited up for battle. The path was chosen for me may be different for you, I was very stubborn and rebellious.

It was on the road to Damascus when everything changed in my life, while traveling thru three around 1:00 am, waking me out of a deep sleep "now is the time to leave" I didn't want to question the Spirit of the Living God because I already knew what his voice sound like, since this wasn't my first experience hearing God speak audible in the way where you know it's real from Heaven. Not sure how to make the journey I begin packing my personal items after a day or so I wasn't moving fast enough when I was instructed to just take what I can fit in the Van put it in Storage and leave immediately. Now fear is beginning to come over me as to why I should leave a place that I have reside for twenty-five years.

The Spirit of the Living God informed me that it was the case I was fighting; he used me to exposed spiritual wickedness in high places. The Boeing Company was doing something that was unethical, the cover-up went for years. Apparently it was a ring of Law Attorneys including a Judge; they decided to cause more injury that to acknowledge their wrong-doing. Apparently forgot or didn't believe in the God and the cries of innocent blood appeared before our God. Innocent people who have died or been injured suffered and God got the Glory, the people will benefit what the perpetrator didn't want them to know the truth.

And God blessed them and God said unto them, Be fruitful, and multiply, and replenish the earth, and subdue it: and have dominion over the fish of the sea, and over the fowl of the air, and over every living thing that moveth on the earth. Genesis 1:28

The company could no longer cover-up the injustice. Once the spirit of darkness received the word I'm aware of his device, it became unreal I was being followed everywhere, then monitored on phone conversations. At least ten investigators were run out of the neighbor, by the police department. All I heard throughout the night was sirens from the police cars. I lived in a quiet neighborhood so I knew this was very unusual, my first though was I'm out of here, will follow the Lord wherever he lead.

Suddenly, from out of nowhere this whirl of wind came and filled the apartment. It was Shechinah Glory. I immediately fell to my knees and began giving God Worship and Praise, saying word like "Lord I trust you and only you, I know that your protection surrounds my very being" then I went into the unknown tongue and stay there for a good length of time.

Leaving Washington State in the beginning of winter January 25, 2013 and crossing the Rocky Mountains to reach a destination that only God knew would end my journey. I had no idea where the Spirit was leading me but I was being direct into unfamiliar territory. My initial thought was "Jesus you are my Shepard, and I'm the Sheep who will follow wherever you lead. I can say the experience of the scriptures on having no home after being uprooted from my convert zone.

He that dwelleth in the secret place of the most High shall abide "under the shadow of the Almighty. Psalm 91:1

I will say of the Lord, He is my refuge and my fortress; my God; in him will I trust. Psalm 91:1

He shall cover thee with his feathers, and under his wings shalt thou trust; his truth shall be thy shield and buckler. Psalm 91:4

I was happy where I was in Jesus Christ he kept proving himself more and more each day; I found a resting place under the shadow of the most High God. Jesus made me feel honored to receive the calling that he has chosen, moving on his spoken words, when operating under the spirit you can only receive Jesus Christ message if you are connected with him. You can only enter through the Spirit.

That which is born of the flesh is flesh; and that which is born of the Spirit is spirit. St. John 3:6

God is Love; his spirit is about Love for there is no respect of person, he treats me no different than he treats anyone else, Jesus died for all mankind, and he Love's everybody even when some don't love him.

The fruit of the spirit Jesus is more valuable than Silver and Gold. I knew in my heart this day would come because I had *ve* confidence in the Holy Spirit and the confirmation from the *Holy* Spirit. Although I share everything Jesus put in my spirit, *one* really believed. If it was something supernatural that *had* dropped in my spirit with confirmation they would be *afraid* and stay far away from me. I'm thankful for my *because* they believe in sticking together as a family, altho *they would* talk among themselves, not make any conclusio *what has* happened supernaturally. Not knowing that the *were afraid to* some supernatural incidents in their own liv *experiencing speak on the supernatural. Whenever they did it was always shared with me of their supernatural occurrences for reassurance. I will always give them what Jesus would give me; they would receive it and meditate on it. If it comes to pass I never hear anything else, and if it doesn't come to pass then it's back to Jesus as to what did happen. They never doubt the Holy Ghost Power and they would communicate with each other as family should and come to their own conclusion. They would end it with "don't tell her", you will never hear the end of it, but what they didn't know is that Jesus would allow me to hear the conversations anyway. After years of being hurt with their cruel talking about me in the supernatural, I would hear conversations in the supernatural that would pierce my heart and cause me to shut down. I wasn't prepared to acknowledge the gift that the Lord Jesus had given; it took a long time for me to accept my gifts. I would run away but Jesus was always there with loving arms, stretched out to comfort me from my own fears. Now, the Lord Jesus has equipped me with knowledge, and understanding including wisdom as a key element of being acceptable to the calling. Not allowing the enemy to overthrow his plan with deception to his people, sharing how to activate the spiritual supernatural powers through the empowerment of Jesus Christ. I Love Jesus so much that my decision was to walk in the fruits of the spirit, and share his Love with everyone he places on my path.*

> *Love, Joy, Peace, Longsuffering, Gentleness, Goodness, Faith, and Meekness Temperance against such there is no law. Galatians 5:22-23*

Spiritual vs Religion

It's very important to have a relationship with God knowing him as your Heavenly Father, with the knowledge of being aware of spiritual warfare in high places. From the beginning of God's creation he was inspired to give man a life of truth and understanding with his plan and purpose for their journey on earth. Lucifer also has a plan and purpose for men.

> For we wrestle not against flesh and blood, but against principalities, against powers, against the rulers of the darkness of the world, against spiritual wickedness in high places. Ephesians 6:12

In the beginning God created Lucifer, he being the most beautiful archangel was full of wisdom, the minister of music conducting the worship. Satan wanted to equal to God eventually taking over the Kingdom using God's creation against the purpose of what it was designed to accomplish. Because of Satan pride he fell from grace, the great dragon was cast out. God cast him into the earth from heaven.

> And there was war in heaven: Michael and his angels fought against the dragon; and the dragon fought and his angles, and prevailed not; neither was their place found any more in heaven. And the great dragon was cast out, the old serpent, called the Devil, and Satan, which deceiveth the whole

world; he was cast out into the earth, and his angels were cast out with him. Revelation 12:7-9

Before his great fall he took one-third of the angels with him devising tactics such as bringing false accusations, being the oppressors who use authority unfairly to persecute the woman and all of mankind. Satan had great anger for mankind, because he knew that he only had but a short time on earth.

God created another plan that would defeat the enemy that would disarm him from his powers, bringing him down into the bottomless pit where him and his demons will remain until eternity. This would be the emphases of the book knowing that Satan will be defeated and God has won the victory.

Being on fire for the Lord he will give you a life worth living, take the old life and replace it with a new life that is separate from the familiar, the renewal of the mind. When God open your spiritual eye, you can look beyond their faults and see the need, but you must be led by the spirit, so you don't get caught up in a cult, such as; the Jim Jones era (share the experience of the feeling from the recorded tape), not following behind every wind a doctrine for it is only going to last a short period of time.

The spirit of the living God is internal opens your spiritual ear to hear what the spirit has to say. Getting to know his spirit is the trust you have established between your Heavenly Father, and he will trust you. Trusting in the Lord God is the ultimate step on getting to know him, believing in what his spirit has to say and knowing that it is truth.

Supernatural Power's

There is a natural body, and there is a spiritual body. 1 Corinthians 15:44

Jesus Christ has empowered all saints by shedding his blood on the Cross; we must now learn how to operate in his Glory thru the power of the Holy Spirit, to be used by the Almighty God with his Supernatural Power. All assignments are generated thru the power of the Holy Ghost; only the true Power. The power of the Holy Ghost is what some people are searching for but only a few will ever be able to obtain, the true power comes only through Jesus Christ to receive the spiritual power of God. You must have a covenant with the Almighty God then we are his Sons and Daughters with everlasting life.

Except a man be born of water and of the Spirit, he cannot enter into the Kingdom of God. John 3:5

There is neither Jew nor Greek, there is neither bond nor free, there is neither male nor female; for ye are all one in Christ Jesus. Galatians 3:28

In the present of the spirit is no place for fear in the supernatural ream, it will be different than anything you can imagine. The things that were supernatural appeared as supernatural so there is no confusion as to what spirit the world is operating because of access to both worlds. In the beginning it was him calling my name, mostly small messages. The time came when I was to pick up the mantel but because of my selfishness not wanting to give my entire life to God making statements that the cross was too heavy. I got in big trouble with the Holy Ghost, I never felt God anger like I did the day he visited my apartment. Found myself a resting place in Jesus". Things are extremely clearer now, since endurance and acceptance I have learned through the wisdom of the Holy Spirit. Thankful to have been chosen to share the gifts of the spirits, which you may know Jesus has empowered me with gift of insight into supernatural, and he can do the same for you. Being equipped with power from Jesus Christ gives your ability to operate above atmosphere in high places; this gift is more precious than silver and gold.

Jesus Christ hath saved us, and called us with a Holy calling, not according to our works, but according to his own purpose and grace, which was given us in Christ Jesus before the world began. 2 Timothy 1:9

Trust in the Lord with all thine heart; and lean not unto thine own understand. Proverbs 3:5

We as a people of God must learn not to lean on our own understanding when you are led by the spirit you must Trust God completely, in other words we have to walk in blind Faith, where we can't see our way like a blind man.

Most people in life have a plan to go in their own directions, but in the spirit of the Lord becomes our steps, for they have been order by the Lord Jesus. His plan becomes our plan then we are no longer our own person. The harvest is plenty and not enough willing workers, after they have been cleanse by the blood of the lamb most just sit and become fat calf's but Christianity is more than just a fatten calf. People are suffering and looking for answers, when they manage to get at the house of the Lord, most are greeted with saint's who have their own issues they are not concerned about no one else agenda, but we as Christian have an obligation. Our Lord Jesus Christ that has empowered us to complete his purpose and plan for this world.

> The spirit of the Lord God is upon me; because the Lord hath anointed me to preach good tidings unto the meek; he hath sent me to bind up the brokenhearted, to proclaim liberty to the captives and the opening of the prison to them that are bound. Isaiah 61:1

We need to get away from hurting God's people, some are the ones that pray for world changes, return to your first Love which is Jesus Christ who raise his people for such a time in this season. The gift is not easily achieved I went thru many trials and tribulations, I had to overcome the ones that I didn't do well with try it again a repeated test, but through it all Jesus was with me all the way. I had to go through some of the trials and tribulations example; the ability to deal with annoying people, for years various stages of testing of patience, because I was in the natural and felt that it would be easier to cut them off stop wasting my time. God being God seen a deeper potential in this young woman. If someone comes into contact with the Spirit of the Living God, they're not always aware enough to identify the Spirit of the Living God. If they do they become aware jealous become the root, then person that God is using has this battle.

In the bible there was a certain man named Simon who saw the apostles lay their hands on a person after they were baptized. Then the person received the gift of the Holy Ghost, was given to those who believed. Simon said "give me also this power, that on whomsoever I lay hands on he may receive the Holy Ghost he "offered them money". But Peter said "thy money perish with thee", because you thought that the gift of the Holy Ghost can be purchased with money. His heart was not right and Peter told him to repent.

> For I bear them record that they have a zeal of God, but not according to knowledge. For they being

ignorant of God's righteousness and going about to establish their own righteousness, have not submitted themselves unto the righteousness of God. Romans 10:2-3

So many people want this power from on high but your heart must be right in the sight of God, you cannot have a lot of the world's care in your spirit. Your mind has to be made up to become a servant of God. If their unable to obtain the power of the Holy Spirit from God, they will go and initiate and start a false power and pretend it's the original Holy Ghost.

If you look closely nothing happens, only having a form of power.

A certain of the vagabond Jews exorcists, took upon themselves to call over them which had evil spirits the name of the Lord Jesus whom Paul preached. And there were seven sons of one Sceva a Jew and chief of the priest, the evil spirits answered and said Jesus I know, and Paul I know but who are you? The man with the evil spirit was leaped on them and overcame them, and prevailed against them, so they fled out of the house naked and wounded. Acts 19:13-16

For men shall be lovers of their own selves, covetous, boasters, "proud," blasphemers, "disobedient to parents, unthankful, unholy, "Without natural affection, "trucebreakers, "false accusers, "incontinent, fierce, despisers of those that are good, "Traitors, heady, highminded, "lovers of pleasures more than lover of God;

Having a form of godliness, but denying the power thereof: "from such turn away. 2 Timothy 3:2-5

When God gives you the keys to enter his Kingdom there are many mansions in the kingdom, many keys but you must know which key open which door. The Supernatural doors where all the mysteries of

God are kept, inside is all supernatural power. He has to trust you before he will reveal his supernatural power to anyone. Remember God trusted the devil and he tried to get away with God's Devine plan, but God is God and he will not allow anyone to disrupt his creation or have dominion over the Kingdom. God said "I'm a jealous God" before him was none? Since God already knows what's in our heart, he knew us before we were in our mother womb. I want everyone to know that I really tried to share what the Lord has given me for years and I loved to testify about his Supernatural Powers, not knowing that one day the Spirit of the Lord would stop me from speaking, no longer to be a witness about any of the mysteries of God's divinity in the supernatural. My testimonies would change from God's supernatural powers to giving Thanks and Praise unto the Lord. When I was no longer speaking about what the Lord had placed in my spirit he had me to write them down, things began to change around the church. The people that were my friends in the church turned out to become irritated, then the entire church was discontented and against me. They would call me all types of names soon it got even worst, when they tried to catch me on fire, saying I was the devil. I was very confused not knowing that my words were being written, and sold for a profit against my knowledge. When I would come for prayer they would start pleading and rebuking me as the devil, and I knew I did not have one evil bone in my body. Of course I went to my heavenly father wounded and dismayed; he always comforted me and showed me the meaning for the attacks until I became an overcomer in Jesus Christ.

I learned the true meaning of forgiveness and I would have to forgive from the heart. This was part of his divine plan to strengthen me not to be judgmental and to love everyone even my enemies. God knew what was going on in the heart, and if anything appeared in my heart I would have to say "cleanse me" again Jesus, "renew the right spirit" so I can do your will. When I would humble myself before the Almighty God with my broken heart, saying "I'm just trying to be his servant", each time I get up from my knees praying Jesus would always give me more power. This would enable me to stay in the fight longer as a good soldier and endure until the end. God always rewarded me with something that I wasn't expecting and it would be very good, because he only knows how to give good gifts to his children. It was good for me that I have been afflicted; that I might learn thy statutes, only God himself could have done this marvelous work so you can't help but give him praise. The moment that I had a made up mind to stay where God had placed me on my walk with him, it is when Jesus who blessed me with a song "I Got a Made up Mind" for an entire year, soon as the words were penetrating out of my heart, more assignments begin to flourish in my life. As I accept each assignment without any murmur or hesitation it was my own personal relationship with my Heavenly Father and he knew me. Then Jesus would place in my spirit to stand up and be bold and speak about what I have told you in the spirit. I was very shy in public speaking and still today I don't enjoy public speaking, but then suddenly the Holy Ghost would actually help me overcome this hindrance. I would get this big wind behind me which pushes me up onto my feet, as I'm standing there looking around like what had just happened, whosoever is conducting the praise and worship service would say go ahead sister Linda when I open my mouth, these words would just flow out like water and with power from on high. Then when I have said everything the Spirit of the Lord would tell me go home, and I would sleep like a new born baby very relaxed and peaceful. Your Trust builds even more on every side of life you trust God no matter what the circumstance may be. I would share this information with other saint's they would only think of me as some crazy person and become fearful and stay far away from me I lost many friends and even some family, eventually after being able to overcome the test through my Faith in God, knowing it will be alright at the end. The more tests that God has sent me through, the more I overcame I found myself walking alone with fewer friends. You don't have to ask them to leave or separate yourself from them, because the Power of the Holy Ghost will determine that for you, especially when he has a greater work for you to accomplish. I had plenty of friends, I was very popular and my family loved me dearly, they would say "She is Wise". You can ask her anything and it would work or close enough. That would be their conclusion of me. The jealousy started and I couldn't understand but it was all part of God's process to get me where he wanted me to be, on the spiritual level, not always seeing things from a natural point of view. I stayed humble and never allow my mouth to mummer about what was going to happen next. I was connected and no one else was could understand, instead I would be more thankful to God for my trials and tribulations. I would welcome any problems or obstacles and would be excitedly glad, not really understanding why I was glad. I even took it one step further I would go to my family and friends to assist them with their supernatural power giving the advice to them resolve their problems.

I was always concerned about the things of God and I believed in his power, especially during the time my mother was exercising her Faith in the Supernatural Power's of the Living God. God kept me around as a witness to the operation of the Supernatural Power working in her life. My mother also passed all her test, trial's and tribulation's she would say to me "I have pleased my Father" I would ask her what do you mean Mother that was so pleasing to your Father. My mother would continue speaking of her Faith and she would just stay in her bible and pray. I would pray with her most out of all of her children, this was because I wanted to know what caused her to become so joyful about Jesus, and how could I please God. Then the Lord would give to me some segments of his power and I would go to my mother with excitement trying to explain to her what God had just revealed to me in the spirit. This particular time was my first experience when the Lord showed me his Shechinah Glory and I ran as far as I could being afraid, my mother would say it is God's divine presence in the Supernatural, you have seen his glorious light. This would give her strength to minster to me for hours, watched her being so compassionate to the things of God, and for the people of God really enlightened me to walk by Faith and not by sight. It took me years on how to operate in the power our Heavenly Father I spent a lot of that time running from his spirit. Today I know how God feels about his people and the unsaved ones that haven't made a decision to come into the body of Christ he love them even more. I know that sometimes we want to judge people and say who should be the one to accept Jesus Christ, I heard many saint's make that statement because they have the Holy Ghost and God has given them the authority. But to judge according to the bible, I believe a lot of it is done in the flesh and God has nothing to do with making sinners feel awkward, for some reason Christians put themselves above God's little ones making themselves rulers. When you hurt God's little ones it takes the Lord to motivate that person again to ever be part of the body of Christ or they create their own God. All because in their mind they were offended by one of God's representative, why would they want to be part of that body of God when he enjoys hurting people? Not until Jesus has to bring them closer, to get their attention usually reaches deep into the heart.

> Therefore, said I unto you, that no man can come unto
> me, except it were given unto him of my Father. St.
> John 6:65

I believe during the deliverance process some of the saint's personality is not all transformed as Paul says we overcome daily, if you have anger problems it will come out in the works that you do, if you have judgmental problems it will also be revealed. When you're working with God's people you have to be very careful with the saint's and especially the little ones they have no defense, your power in the Holy Ghost intimidate them when all this should be done in Love.

Behold, I send you forth as sheep in the midst of wolves;
"be ye therefore wise as serpents, and 'harmless" as
doves. St. Matthew 10:16

When a person comes to you and God reveals to you their circumstances, and tell you they are broken in pieces knowing how the enemy has tossed them to and fro remember those are the little ones. Our heart should feel Love enough to want them released from the enemy clenches, because when they reach that Plato in Jesus no one can take the credit but God. Many times Bishops, Pastors, Missionary's where their crown on earth, you better honor them because of who they are, with the power and authority from God. There are no titles in the Supernatural and in Heaven we all will be worshipping and praising the Living God day and night. Some will receive their crown of Glory and a Robe, for being victorious by overcoming Satan. This does not make any one above another God has no respect of person, we will give Praise and worship to the King of Kings, and Lord of Lords it will be about his Shechinah Glory.

In spite of everything else without Jesus, we all would be lost; it was his blood that was shed on Calvary. We have gotten so complacent in our walk for God that it just another day's journey, it's more than that when our expectancy is waiting for the second coming of Jesus Christ. Each year he delays his second coming. We have a dilemma to adjust, not to get the work done focused on planting seeds of success. If all the saint's would have been doing their works the world crises would not have gotten out of control, our enthusiasm to please God has changed to only interest in greed of money, not concerned about the suffering of the people in our own environment. Now God has made changes to change the world and most believe when we get to this point God is coming back to end society in 2012, if it does only because man has become a disappointment to God's creation. All we need sometimes is to make a change in our own life for Jesus Christ. Why did Jesus always escape to the other side, making adjustment on where God want him to go next? We need to go on the other side to adjust with the Lord's expectation, so our generations don't focus on the world coming to an end, but find their purpose in the Kingdom of God. The world is in a difficult crisis has ever seen it like this before, people are looking for answers but the questions are still unanswered. Until you have had a Spiritual Encounter with the Spirit of the Living God we will wander around blaming other's for the downfall of America. We have to get things together because our next generation has no interest in the God we serve; they want the money and the power. I hate to be the one who bust your bubble, when the end take place your money and power will have no value. The only value will be your soul; if you did not make any investment it has no value. So wise up and get to know your God with omnipotent powers, reach for world changes to stop human suffering. We talk about Kingdom work and some are vigilantly on their assignments but we need the majority to make Heavenly decisions.

I can remember testifying to the church saying majority of our young people are following the doctrine that speaks against the God of their parents, teaching them to choose their own belief which forces them to believe in evolution. Parents should have been tearing down that Spirit of the anti-Christ, instead they went about their daily activities, and now the dogma has become acceptable and has taken control of our next generation. If we don't come together and pray this demon out, using the Holy Ghost power that God has already given to every believer. Exercise your empowerment, get it out of the next generation or they will be affected by that same demonic spirit for generation to generations. Now that demonic spirits have become more empowered through the church organization, our next move is utilizing the Supernatural Power. We can delay the destruction of the world thru God's mercy and bring back America. Let us do what we should as followers of Jesus keeping God's creation going until his second coming; the world would be destroyed by man and his machines if we do nothing but murmur. We all can stand for America to improve the future for your children and grandchildren; my way of sharing what the Lord has placed in my heart is written in books series. Maybe, if the attacks from the church would not have happened I would still be doing things the same way, God has given me the permission to write the series of books that has been placed in my spirit. When the Lord gives me something I sample it out on my family first, then the spirit tells me where to go from there. Search your spirit with the Living God ask for your assignment to change our world, the more involved the more power. Most people just want to live in this world and not make any waves, but I say make waves it's for your children and your children's children, your response will affect the next generation. Being called by God gives you honorary privileges to operate in his Supernatural Powers. If you utilize it accordingly, and then God would trust you with his most secrete words. Whenever you are doing something that is pleasing to Our Heavenly Father his words are life similar to food for the body, more than anything in this world so do a great job for him. When the assignment was placed in my spirit, I was a little nervous because I didn't have the education needed to write such books and when my God reinsured me that he will place his words in my spirit I stood on Faith and began the assignment with gladness.

In the series of books I will be sharing a lot of information generally how I was able to reach God in the Supernatural, this is something that I have been sharing with church leaders for years, some feel that I should only release this to the church, but God has given me authorization, place his written words into series of books for all who believe in the Supernatural Power's of God.

> He that believeth on me as the scripture hath said "out of his belly shall flow rivers of living waters" St. John 7:38

Verily, verily, I say unto you; He that believeth on me,
the works that I do shall he do also, and greater works
that these shall he do; because I go unto my father. St.
John 14:12

Over the years of testimonies and praying for the individuals that
God would place on my path, I shared everything God had placed
in my spirit about the Supernatural Power's of the Living God.
What the Lord spoke in my spirit the people wouldn't respond
with very much with enthusiasm, until they saw his Supernatural
Power's work and a miraculous event occur. Fear would rise up
within them and they would say I don't want to know anymore,
or they just shut down automatically. Although some church leaders
feel that the power should be given to the church leaders only, they
would try to control what happened when the supernatural power
operated. This is found in some of the bad churches, where the spirit
of the Living God does not dwell. Some church leaders would get
the information slap their name on it and use it as their own. It
was not fine with me; it was given by the Living God which was
dropped in my spirit. If they would be more obedient, maybe God
could trust them with his supernatural power. Instead I rather share
with the young generation who has become lost in the word of God.
Whenever I would share with the unsaved people in the church it
became an issue. They felt God's word was for their children only, in
my heart God was for all mankind not just for the selected.

When the Spirit of the Living God words came true, then
Christians people would somewhat believe, never ask any question
on how to reach the higher levels in Jesus, but rather going about
life as if the Supernatural Power doesn't exist. If there were any
questions they would sneak around to get the answers, following
me or even placing church members as detectives on my path,
attempting hacking my computer for this book. Nevertheless, exclude
any consultation in seeking God's advice, on how to receive the
Supernatural Power but rather pretend that they are operating
with the power. Jesus wants true believers, not as if you already

know what is going on, but willing to learn God's process. Once the conversations began about the Supernatural Powers there's this look of fear on their faces, and you don't want to see that look on people you care about.

> For God hath not given us the spirit of fear; but of power, and of love, and of a sound mind. II Timothy 1:7

I learn to only speak when God tells me, or minister the word of God with someone when God instructs me to do so. When it comes to my family they get whatever flows from the spirit. Most would just listen and have no comment; if they're concerned about something that needs to be corrected they just accept the correction. At times, they separate from me and I would have to be the one to make the first contact. It is a lonely place to be when you have the gift of supernatural powers. No one can understand what the next message is so they're careful not to interrupt the spirit, when it comes upon me knowing that I would never use God's gift in a negative way.

In reality there are two types of Supernatural Powers, one that belong to Satan and another that is controlled by God. The Holy Ghost some prefer to call it the Holy Spirit as the highest power, Satan's power is beneath. The Power of the Living God that was determined when Satan wanted to be equal to God, because of his pride he fell from Grace and was cast out of Heaven into the earth. That is what the power of the Living God did to him, on that day and he took one-third of the angels with him, they were defeated. God has disarmed him from his powers, and given it to the people of God. The Supernatural Power from the Living God the Holy Ghost is the originated power that comes from Our Heavenly Father, no one came duplicate his power, it is real as it gets.

Now the power in the world is very small because God gave man power over Satan and so he is limited, he doesn't want anyone to know, Satan continues demanding control over people with the belief that he still has the power. When he activates his power in the Supernatural everyone gives him more credit that he deserves, he is only a Spirit that is limited to the Supernatural Power's of the Living God which operates in every Christian that believes and is not afraid. If you have the power from the Holy Ghost then Satan can't overpower you, he definitely can't deceive you because the Supernatural Power is activated. Put Satan under your feet, which then causes him to break into little pieces and have to start all over again. The negatives in the world today have given Satan more power than he was design to have, if you change the way you view the Supernatural Power and put all your Faith and Trust in the Lord Jesus, God can elevate you into the powerful level where Satan must obey. The main ingredient is obedience to God's instructions; most will start with agreement but soon depart. This will place you where Satan knows your identity and you won't endure, you have been identified with a ranking. When you operate in the Supernatural Powers you can't have any Fears once the enemy discovers that you are fearful he will run you out of town, and show you things that your mind will not be able to comprehend. Because it's the supernatural the enemy can change objects to appear different than what it supposes to be, the same with the spiritual supernatural. So you really have to rely on the Power of the Holy Ghost in the supernatural world, the spiritual world knows that you are of human form. Jesus gave us the power to operate in the supernatural, and then you have the same accessible as all other beings in the spirit world. When you get involved with the supernatural your mind has to be made up completely, there cannot be any doubts about who you are in Jesus Christ. If you release any thing doubtful everything can turn bad. Some people in the Church thought I didn't know who I was in Jesus because of the power God has given, they would set me up without my knowledge. They summoned me to the Jurisdiction Headquarters' in Washington State where all the Bishops, Pastors and Missionaries would have me perform my spiritual gifts on someone that they had chosen, just to prove to themselves if the power was real. I say I don't owe anyone an explanation, my approval was from my Heavenly Father, in the Supernatural world where I am known by my spiritual name, which was given by my Heavenly Father. Jesus has ordained me to move about the earth to preach the acceptable year of the Lord.

> The spirit of the Lord is upon me, because he hath anointed me to preach the gospel to the poor; he hath sent me to heal the brokenhearted, to preach deliverance to the captives, and recovering of sight to the blind, to set at liberty them that are bruised. Luke 4:18

I could imagine when the Pharisee's questioned Jesus and they were not getting the answers that they expected they hung him on a tree, it was lack of understanding on their part. I really didn't like talking about things of the supernatural that people don't believe, but the ones who say they believe really don't even scratch the surface of the unknown supernatural power. This can be somewhat scary to those who don't understand. But if God gives you the power you must exercise it exactly as he instructs or you will become spiritually dead and that's not good. There is no cure for spiritual death in this world because your body will still be here on earth and your mind will be where ever they bury the spirits. The spirits comes in many different shapes and forms; it depends on which form you will be operating out of, God uses me in spiritual for battles that need transformation. God has assigned a host of wartime angels because the demons are very clever, their ranks are as General's in an army. Example; when you cast off demons out of a person on earth, what is actually going on is the spirits don't want to come out of that person. The power of the Holy Ghost that is operating in the believer and is doing the casting out to remove a demon and they know they're being controlled by the Holy Ghost. When the demons come out they have to find a warm body to continue on earth, and if they don't then it is lights out for them, their leader Lucifer will eliminate them for not doing their job, they go into the spiritual death mode. But if they find a warm body then they can continue on earth and operate as their leader instructs them. Many times I would hear saint's when they casting out demons say "Go back to the pit of Hell where you come from" this statement is inaccurate because they can't go there until their time is up here on earth. Everything has been planned according to Jesus death, that's why when you call on the name Jesus the demons must flee, and it doesn't matter who says it, the power is in the name. But if you try to cast out demons in the name of Jesus and you are not qualified, that's when they have the power over you because you haven't been authorized to operate on that level. Once Jesus gives you the Key to operate on the level of the supernatural then every demon knows who you are, and they also know how much power you are operating with, and they will try to use various tactics to make you a non-believer of the power that Jesus has given you. In other words you must be stable with you walk with God, you can't go to the left nor to the right, you have to stay on the path that God has provided. The instructions on how to win the battle comes from the Spirit of the Living God, and your spiritual ear has to be open to receive the information or you will not be able to work with the Supernatural Powers correctly to make an impact, and you must keep all of the details to yourself and only share the victory of Jesus.

Most people want to know how to access the Supernatural Power's but it's God doing, he's the one who chooses the individual to become the vessel to operate, and not always he will use a clean vessel like many of the saint's believe he does according to what will get the victory, he's God almighty and he can use whomever he wants, all power belong to God. If for some reason he uses you, please don't' get the earthy flesh going with the Spirit of Pride it won't be long-lasting, that is one thing God hates when it comes to his power. Always keep in mind this is God's creation, and his alone. If anyone thinks that they can operate in God's power and focus the attention to themselves it will not happen, you will not be used as a vessel for

God. Beside he already knows what's in your heart and he knows your intentions before the thought can even reach the brain.

Nevertheless, your heart and mind must be pure enough for the Lord to speak to you about his plan and purpose, and then he will instruct you on how to carry out the mission. Once the trust has been established between you and God things get even deeper with the supernatural. God can use you to help develop or cleanup an effected world; because God knows that the enemy is out to get his subjects at any cost. Because of the anger he has against God, so this battle has nothing to do with us it something the enemy has against God. The Lord will do whatever to protect his people. He Loves us so much, and that's why he sent Jesus his only begotten son, that the world through him may be saved. No one knows the hour of the second coming of Jesus but I know that when the trumpet blows it's going to be loud enough to wake the dead. Many people of God speak about the second coming but really have not seen the aftermath, it is not godly to speak on things that you have not experienced, and the images of who God is and what he look like is a myth in this atmosphere. The spirit is not what most people would be able to digest, his Shechinah Glory illuminates the entire surroundings so you are unable see God, like looking at the sun close up.

My name was called by the angel and I watched him enter into our atmosphere and I watched him leave our atmosphere, the sound was so loud that it made me tremble, the windows of my vehicle was vibrating. This wasn't the only time I heard the loud voice, when he visited me with anger that was very frightening.

The atmosphere in the Supernatural world is very large, the angels are large, the mansions are large, the trees extra-large, the river large, everything was large and it was in order. My God is a God of order so all of this confusion on earth will discontinue and not be there. All the different denominations no longer exist; it will be only *where we all desire to give Praise and Honor to the most High God. There will be no color barrels, so my suggestion is to get it together here on earth. Now I can understand why the path will be narrow, because a lot of saint's will miss Heaven if they don't change their way of thinking, Love is the key to a path in Jesus Christ, but it is not the key to the Supernatural world; like I said there are many keys, you need the key that unlocks the Supernatural, and you must get the key from Jesus. Once he gives it to you seek out which key unlocks the door, because not every key unlocks the door you want to enter, unless Jesus gives you the master key. Before all of that he will already had instructed you as to why you have been chosen to do the assignment. At that level God will not hold your hand, and there are no provision made in your honor so you must know because you know. Your Faith is strong and not wimpy; to have the Faith that God is with you all the way. It is the beginning of a journey that you can't really explain so that people here on earth will not understand. I can say that he has a place prepared and it's nothing like those imagines that people claim. Once in a while when I see that I say, why they would create a graven image when the Bible says we are not to do such a thing. God's thoughts are higher than our thoughts, what God wants is that we all make it to the kingdom, because Hell was not designed for his people, but thru disobedience we can easily be cast into the Hell fire with Satan and all his demons. So I say believe even if it seems impossible since the end result you will have to have the Faith anyway, to sustain the supernatural events. I notice that most in the next generation, have no knowledge of the supernatural powers of Jesus as my personal savior. I believe that it will be devastating if this continues because the next generations behind them will be completely lost.*

Generally people expect you to have the knowledge on how to operate in the Supernatural; this isn't something that you would give instructions on because everyone doesn't believe in the Supernatural. Most people think like they speak saying "I believe" although you should have made some sort of contact with the supernatural if it is only in visions and dreams. The majority people want everything on a silver platter or microwaveable, it takes a lot to work under the power of the Holy Ghost, to identify when and who knows which Spirit is speaking and which Spirit is operating with powers. Not just having the ability to move mountains but to take that mountain, and place it outside the camp.

In the Supernatural a person first must understand what goes on in the spiritual world, there is no room for fear; if you are fearful in this world then the next world would make you crazy. God's Supernatural Power's is more advanced than what the natural mind can comprehend; we are used to the normal ways of life in this world as to how it operates, and the functions which take us from day to day. We are living in the natural while trying to advance to the supernatural, in our surrounding things changes drastically, when the environment has gone into another dimension. It's nothing like the movies; some vague imagination that has been created in the human sense, the supernatural is so real that when you speak things began to take form and shape immediately. Getting use to the environment before you can really manifest in the operations of spiritual activities, being familiar with super large angels, noise so loud that it echoes like thunder, hearing conversations without the mouth moving, and so much more yet no fear exist. After your mind has been programmed to call things as they are then the real substance begins to work in the supernatural world, you learn to speak things in the now for supernatural powers to operate. When I first begun I must say it would leave me stunned with blank thoughts of what had just happened, although I didn't have any doubts or fears I was taken by the fascination that this is something that has never been revealed to me in any shape or form. As I continue to grow in God's Supernatural Powers from Our Lord Jesus Christ, each step was different from the last, always something new and rewarding. Never could I say this was boring, it was very interesting. As time went forward and I saw more and more activities of the Supernatural Powers of the Living God my

Faith began to grow and put things together, noticing the outcome was positive. Whenever there was a negative outcome I would always go back to my Heavenly Father for advice on how to make the corrections, this was an ever learning process. In the natural you can reach certain heights in this world then you have to change to another program, but in the supernatural world it just keeps going and going as long as you have the energy to pursue. I was always a curious person who wanted more than what the natural eye can see, with the natural eye things are what you see is what you get, but in the Supernatural it can change at any given moment. When I would look up into the sky as a child, it just seemed more than what meets the natural eyes, definitely couldn't see myself as the average person in life. When the first man landed on the moon it was really impressive to me because I knew in my spirit that something more was out there than just space. I believe what was placed in my heart as a child; it kept my curiosity going until I grew up.

Now I can say God's creation is real and not some scientific research. If you listen to science we were not created by God it happens to be a lie from Satan himself. When the end time comes for the truth to be revealed Satan's identity as him ruling the world, many would have been deceive by his deceptions already, not believing God for his word as the creator. I wouldn't want to live my life under false pre-tense, just as the bible speaks "try every spirit to see if it to be real". I wanted the true and Living God and all that he has to offer me; I was planning on keeping myself before the Throne of Grace until I get my answers. After my mother passed away at a young age it left me with many questions for God, and I can say he has answered each one, in return I grew closer to him and learned how to receive his power.

This book is not a step by step method on how to receive God's power, it's not my power to allocate, but I can tell you how to position yourself to obtain the power, if God perceive you're qualified according to his purpose. If the Lord Jesus has a need for you to work within the power of the Holy Ghost, then Jesus only can provide you with assignments to complete the job. Once I received notification from the Spirit of the Living God, it would dwell in my Spirit; there have been a few occasions where God has spoken audible, sound like thunder roaring and very shattering. I only heard this if I would ignore what the spirit has to say to my spirit, or if I keep doing what I wanted to do which is sin by running away from God as much as possible and not respond. When the spirit does catch up with me and get my attention his speech would shake me up so bad, that I automatically become obedient to whatever he called me to do accordingly. This would go on for the next several years, until I learned to do exactly what the Spirit of the Living God asked usually helping his people. Whenever I would be an unwilling participant, then the Spirit of the Living God would send his angels or power. Only twice I received a visit from him in the Spirit, this would cause me to move quickly. Therefore I would stay humble under the mighty power of the Living God, in other words he would put Fear in me. Now I have accepted all assignments from God, going to him in prayer whenever something is not according to what he has requested. Depending on how the spirit guides me, no more running away. God is in every aspect of my life. Running away from the Spirit only made the circumstances difficult because God has Omni powers. God is everywhere at the same time, there is no place on earth you can run or hide, the Spirit of the Living God was always there.

We all have a part in the body of Christ and sometimes it not always the part you prefer; God gives each of us different gifts which adjust with various people, some have more power than others. Just as the Lord would give you the gift if you do not use God's gift for his glory, the gift you thought you had will no longer exist. Jesus will call you an unprofitable servant and will give your gift to another who will use the gift for the Kingdom of God.

> *But the manifestation of the Spirit is given to every man to profit withal. For to one is given by the Spirit the word of Knowledge, by the same Spirit; To another the working of Faith by the same Spirit; To another the gifts of Healing by the same Spirit; To another the working of Miracles; To another the gifts of Prophecy; To another Discerning of Spirits; To another Divers kinds of tongues; To another the interpretation of Tongues; 1 Corinthians 12: 7-10*

According to the bible there's a difference of administrations, so when God executes this it's because God has an order in which he operate. Even though the bible speaks about how God gives according to the measure of Faith, it has been times when I didn't have Faith and I was told by most missionaries, as well as my mother saying "I will stand on my Faith for you" didn't understand but her faith worked. Now that I have learned to know the Lord Jesus for myself, and realize that it was God's doing to empower me with more power, without asking or seeking that is called Favor. I can say I have a lot of Faith now and believe in the impossible because of where Jesus brought me from; I went thru many trials and tribulations. In addition, suffered through several super storms that Our Lord Jesus Christ brought me out of them all, so where I came from and what I went through with the Spirit of the Living God he has made me who I am today.

To see how the churches would block the people that God wants to use for his Glory, not understanding that he has raised this person just for a specific purpose on earth. Some people in the church have limited understanding about God's expectation of operation of working in the Supernatural Spirit of the Living God. We having incompetency of understanding God's purpose and plan for each individual, that God equipped believers with the Holy Ghost, to accomplish his desired plan through his power for an enriched life. All could be seen is; if you are the favorite person of the church then you have the floor, but if you are not the favorite person then you must sit. The leaders will tell you when the power comes from on high, and they would let you know when it arrives through their own natural sight. This is blocking the flow of the Holy Spirit and of course this would anger God. On the contrary God always has another plan, and sometimes empowers the person more and more until they receive the level of Supernatural Power. They would have to endure hardship as a good soldier, because he wants to bless the people of God. Each time man has a way of grabbing his own blessings, and placing his own tag on it making it to appear as if it's the Spirit of the Living God. The people of God do not receive the Supernatural Power from the Living God since it has been altered, only the power here on earth which is limited. When Jesus Christ has raised up one of his little ones as a child, the people of God become vulnerable and unforgiving, not being merciful towards the raising of the baby saint's, they will injured that individual for personal issues. Then Our Heavenly Father has protected the baby giving a boost of empowerment until they have strength to be used by God.

Similar in my case, the church was growing according to God's plan when the church is blessed the community is blessed, then the nation is blessed, but they interfered in God's original plan, being incapable of saying "please forgive me" they cover up their wrong. Without forgiveness it's over and downhill from there, but they must line up with the Living God and turn this situation back to God. Some of the churches are blessed but the churches that are struggling look at your menu keep the sanctuary uncontaminated.

Because God's power is so real not many people will have access to his Supernatural Power, it is very easy to lose focus as to who really has the power so you must be able to concentrate on the Holy Spirit. Our Lord Jesus Christ defeated the enemy and all power belongs to God the Father, God the Son, and God the Holy Ghost which the Supernatural Power derives from and belongs to the Almighty God. Prior to receiving the power of the Holy Spirit you will be given a course of trials and tribulations in order to prove yourself worthy of the gift; you must be able to pass every examination without being overtaken by the enemy. In other words you must be triumphant in your walk for Jesus Christ conquering the enemy with the right spirit, these set of test are completely different from the trials and tribulation that you would obtain once you receive Jesus Christ as your personal savior. When you walk in the Spirit of the Living God the course can be difficult but not impossible, if I can make it through with little to no Faith anyone who has a made up mind will be able to accomplish their task. Our task the Heavenly Father has bestowed upon each and every Christian according God's purpose and plan for our life to be complete. We being in the natural cannot foresee the purpose of the assignment, the test given by the spirit of the Lord. Nevertheless, through our walk with Jesus Christ we develop a trust in God that no man can detour us from, because we know that all things work together for our good. Jesus only wants us to have the abundant life and sometimes our trials and tribulations are to make us strong. We as Christian must learn to trust Jesus in all aspects of our life that means things seen and unseen, knowing that our Heavenly would not lead us astray, he is the Good Sheppard. Jesus loves his sheep and would leave the 99 and go after the 1, each one of us has a special place in the heart of God. Just when you think that you have reached a plateau in Jesus, that's when he will reveal something else that will automatically causing you to become closer, with questions realizing that you really didn't know what you thought you knew. This begins a new chapter in the journey with Jesus, and before you know it you start to rely on him again and again as if you are still a baby in the Lord. There are so many depths in Jesus you can never get it all at one time, because God is the God of the universe and has All Power in his hands. To really know him you must constantly be ready to step closer and closer to him without any delays or hesitations. If there is any doubt, he will set you aside until you can reach a place of complete trust.

Most Christian does not want to get close to Jesus because they are afraid of the unknown, or they are comfortable. When God becomes your Heavenly Father you trust him in all aspect of your life. Jesus withholds no good thing from his children; he loves us and died for all our sins. Once you understand the Love that Jesus really has for his children then you will no longer pray for material things which only satisfy the flesh to utilize on this planet earth, the supernatural things are external and can be used also here on the planet earth but differently.

> *But my God shall supply all your need according to his riches in glory by Christ Jesus. Philippians 4:19*

We sometimes cut ourselves short of his glory because we do not fully understand how it works, but once God reveals his Shechinah Glory to you everything changes, and the power of the Holy Ghost becomes more real to you in this life as food for the spirit. Your vision of life becomes more of the visible for the world to be a better place and Jesus Loves our earth it's his footstool. His creation will not be done in vain; we all know that God gets the victory at the end, knowing that Satan has been exposed also the Glory of God prior to being kicked out of heaven. Since he knows that he only has but a short time he keeps our minds and our spirit under subjection to this world only to distract us from the universal plan that God really has for his people. Our Heavenly Father loves us so much he will not interfere with our free will, we will have to come to the knowledge of truth ourselves, only a few have actually connected and some have stumble on it such as myself. Of course it's not made vivid so everyone has access but only a few can even get to the level to think outside the box.

Michael the Archangel

I had just left service where the Spirit of the Living God had put me down on the floor, as I fell under the anointing power of the Holy Ghost. I went to eat at a fast food drive thru to get my usual cheeseburger, when suddenly I heard a loud voice, it sounded like it was coming from the sky; someone had called me by name "Linda", the voice had surround sound. Being inside my vehicle the car felt like it was shaken by the voice being so loud, the widow's felt like they would crumple or just bust. I hovered over to guard my eyes in case any glass start flying, then I said very low voice "Who knows me like that"? In a split second I straighten up and Michael the Archangel appeared before the front of the vehicle. As he stood there looking at me and I was looking at him, there was no advancement, when he began to walk forward I was trying to get out of my vehicle. The doors were unlocked but the handle would not release, so I said "I will not take my eyes off you, whatever world you enter into I will be watching you will just have to disappear before my eyes". As I followed him traveling across the parking lot, he was walking very slow and like a commander of something that had a lot of authority, his facial appearance was hardhearted with an unbroken look intently directly at me without any facial expression, such as a Commander. I noticed the traffic light was not changing, there were no cars passing, no people walking, and the atmosphere was as if I were in another dimension. My eyes were astonished to see Michael the Archangel; I was not afraid, more relaxed and wanting to get out the vehicle to communicate. The questions that I wanted to ask him, "Where are you from"? Which I already knew but I wanted to hear it from him, then I asked "Who sent you" and why are you following me"? But that didn't happen because I couldn't open the door, I was trying the entire time the Michael was before my eyes. Just say I was multi-tasking but he continues his journey as I watched him disappear before my eyes. Minutes later everything went back to normal, the traffic light changed, and the vehicles began to pass through and people started moving about their business. I have such vivid description of how he comes across from head to feet; it's been the same each time he gave me the impression of being the Commander, Michael the Archangel with a lot of might as a warrior. He traveled with me everywhere there was going to be trouble and he also protect me from any harm or danger.

Supernatural Encounter's

In my walk with the Lord Jesus I have experienced many spiritual encounters but the Supernatural encounters were placed in a totally different atmosphere. Because you are working in the now, your Faith must have been established by God, that you will never ever detour from his instructions.

When I picked up the mantel that my mother had laid down, I also inherited the Archangel that was assigned to her and became my assigned angel. His name is Michael the Archangel, he is very big and stands about 10-12 feet tall, very powerful as a warrior with confidence, his face is solid with no expressions automatically you know he means business. When he walks things smash to smithereens around him his feet are big and strong, almost like every step it sinks into the ground like it's mud-spattered. When he talks his voice sounds like thunder and lighting, with this roar like lions, you can hear it for miles away. His body is very powerfully built and muscular, his neck was the size of 28" inches. His thighs big very powerful, the size of 40" inches with every muscle detailed, he was a big brawny warrior. Without human intervention you can tell he doesn't fool around with any demons, he takes his assignments very serious just looking upon him brings fear to the brain. Whenever I would see him or he gives me a message I can tell he has a lot of authority, he comes to earth saying and doing what is the assigned and he is gone.

This is the first angel that I have ever met; all other angels received their assignments from the archangel. My mother would describe this angel as one assigned to the family when I was 20 years old. She was very afraid of him; one day the angel said "be not afraid" she said "I'm not afraid anymore". Then one day the angel appears suddenly in front of her, and she went running inside the house she was very frightened. That went on for a while until she was no longer afraid. My brothers would make jokes just to see if they could frighten her again, she would say don't play around with God's angles. We never heard her speak about that angel any more, after her death the angel appeared again.

It wasn't until I met Michael the Archangel was frightening, that's why I would take off running but he would always get there before my arrival. I guess the most frightening part about Michael the Archangel in my encounters would be how sometimes he disguised himself as different humans in life. The reason he transformed his appearance, so I could feel comfortable to communicate with him about messages, or assignments. When he would become visible I was more frightened than when he would just appear suddenly. Compel me take off and run, like I was being chased.

Sometimes the angel and a host of others would have spiritual battles with the demons. I would feel the protection and peace when they would become triumphant. I can say it took years for me to feel comfortable around Michael the Archangel; it's not bad at all when you have an angel that is prevailing on your behalf, then I can really say the battle is not mine.

My first time meeting the Archangel Michael was in Florida, I had been getting spiritual occurrences where my mother would try to direct me into understanding the meaning of supernatural powers. I didn't want to know really; I started running and booked me a ticket I didn't tell anyone that I was leaving, next thing I know she shows up at the airport. The Lord has just begun working in my life; the first time I met an Angel He said "It was Jesus that make you free, you give Jesus the Praise" then he disappeared.

Visit to New Jerusalem

During a Friday night service at church the Holy Ghost came from heaven moving like a rushing mighty wind just flood thru the congregation, and he filled the house and I got caught up in the spirit. This was typical at church the Spirit would dwell at the Temple day and night, all kinds of miraculous things was going on, from healing, deliverance, financial blessings and much more everything was good.

This particular night was very exciting and the Holy Ghost had laid me out, but the congregation was still praising, I could still hear the drum beats fading as I was on the floor. The next thing I was in the spirit ream, Michael the Archangel took my hand and led me up into the midst of the clouds, and we landed on top of God's Holy Mountain. The reason I know my angel is because he was assigned to me, and spoke his name to me, being the only angel that would give me messages. As I was standing there Michael the Archangel was still holding my hand as I was viewing my surroundings, the streets were solid gold it was the first thing I noticed because I could see a reflection of a mirror image of myself and Michael. I follow the street as far as my eyes could see, it got thinner and thinner, and the noise was so loud that it caused me to return my attention back to the New Jerusalem structure. There people inside giving lots of praising and shouting very loud they said "Praise to the King, May Reign Forever and Ever" they kept repeating the same thing over and over again. Then I noticed people in white robes were moving in the spirit towards the New

Jerusalem place of worship, the building was enormous with pillars were solid pearls tall like Redwood Trees but extremely large. The precious gems were imbedded in the wall of the building like decorations, I saw emeralds, topaz, jasper and many more; one gem was the size of a house. And they sparkled like I had never seen before in my life, as I stood there watching with bewilderment I begin to notice the peace that was there and you can feel the Fruits of the Spirit, I felt love, joy, gentleness. Satan was not there, nothing unclean was not even in the atmosphere. Then I wanted to enter into the gates so I looked up at Michael as he let go of my hand, stared at the gates thinking my mother is over there, and my grandmother is there I can see them again. I looked down for a path but nothing just large trees like a forest; I knew there is no way I could get through that I made up my mind to take a chance and go for the run but the visit was over. Michael grabbed my hand and brought me back to earth, as I was returning I could hear the drums again, and people feet were dancing and praising around me as I lay on the floor with my right hand lifted in the air. All I could say when it was over, "who was holding my hand" the members kept saying "no one Sis. Linda, it was just in the air" I was very sad for a few days because I didn't want to come back, that's when Michael the Archangel said you were not ready to enter.

Visit by the Spirit of God

Nearly five years after my mother passed away in 1994 as we were leaving the Paradise Church of God in Christ, California going to the cemetery three people came to me while I was getting into the vehicle, and at different points of time they each said "Who's going to pick up the cross your mother laid down"? I said to the first person "Not me", then the second person came and said the same thing, and again I said "Not me", then the third person came to me and said also "Who's going to pick up the cross your mother laid down"? This time I had gotten frustrated and angry I said "Not me, it's TOO HEAVEY", and that was the reason for my Supernatural visit from the Living God. As I mention five years had passed, and I'm healing from her death going along with my life as usual. The morning that the visit occurred it was around 4:00 am, it had snowed very hard throughout the night, about 3"inches, Everett, Washington. I had a Rottweiler and two cats at the time when the Spirit of the Lord came into my apartment. I was in my bedroom, when suddenly I heard a very loud voice coming from my living room. It sounded like an earthquake but no ground shaking and windows shattering. The voice was angry and very loud saying "This is the day that the Lord has made". About that time I got up out of my bed, as I peeked into the living I could see my dog sitting near the window doing tricks as if someone was there, my cats were being entertained also but in a different location. As the loud voice kept speaking saying "This is the day. . ." about that time I started to run for the window but was unable to open the window, then I ran to the door and couldn't open the door either so I began to panic. At that time the Spirit of the Lord forced me down and I was on my living room floor with my face down and I couldn't move I was bound in the Spirit of the Holy Ghost. Then the voice of the Lord started speaking saying "You my daughter talked about my cross". As I'm there on the floor trying to get up, I began thinking when did I talk about the cross, I was taught not to speak against the cross. The next thought came to my mind saying "I'm going to die". Immediately the Spirit of the Lord eliminated the thought out of my mind. Then another thought came to my mind, "I'm going to have a heart attack", again the Spirit of the Lord eliminated the thoughts. The Sprit of the Lord went on saying "You my daughter talked about my cross, that you know nothing of" again my mind began to roam trying to remember when did I do such a thing like this I know better, then suddenly the Spirit of the Lord removed all thoughts from my mind, it was blank so I could hear the Spirit. He went on say "Your mother bared that cross, your grandmother bared that cross, you my daughter if you do not bared my cross this will be your punishment" the spirit of the Lord went on to say what my punishment will be, he said "I will throw a plague on you, and you will run to every doctor and they will not be able to find nothing wrong with you, then they will throw you into an institution until you die" after that the Spirit of the Lord left, and I was released off the floor. I was severely shaking violently so I grab my dog and put her leash around her neck to go outside to see what had just happened. When I open the door and looked down I seen footsteps on the porch in the snow. Just only one porch were footsteps, and this was disturbing, then my dog would sniff the footprint and look up at me as if she was identifying each foot print, with a bark like she was saying this one was in the apartment. We walked out further and no other footsteps were in the fresh snow that had fallen overnight. I went to the porch and placed my foot inside the footprint and it was a very big footprint so I placed both feet in the footprint and still had a least (3) inches or more that had not been filled by my foot.

Now I'm really nervous because the voice of the Lord was very angry and demanding, and I couldn't stop shaking. I figured that evening I would go to church as a consequence to make it better, as I was driving I couldn't keep my feet on the accelerator I was shaking so hard what normally took (15) minutes to get to church took me (30) minutes I was having trouble driving. When I arrived at church the Pastor said "Daughter are you being obedient to the spirit"? Actually that really shook me even more as I stuttered I said, "Yes I am". Church started and I really praised the Lord like I had never praised him before, I was singing loud and dancing having the best church service of my life. Then I did something imprudent, after church I went up to the Pastor and I wrote a check, I said to the Pastor "I'm going to leave it blank, you can put in whatever amount you want" the pastor said "No daughter you fill in the amount". I left a large amount in the offering and I left and went home everything was great, I was feeling good in my spirit thinking this should reconcile whatever thing I have done wrong. To my surprise (7) days later the voice of the Living God came to me again saying "This is the Day that the Lord has made" I said to myself "he's back" I was so frightened, I stumbled into the living room and was bound in the spirit again, this time the spirit of the Lord said "What is your Answer", and I said "Oh Lord have Mercy on me, Please Forgive Me; I will do whatever you want me to do "now I gave my answer the Spirit of the Living God. He left and I had picked up the Mantel that my mother had laid down, as I have developed maturity with the Lord. My gifts have gone further than what I would have ever expected. God has blessed me so much with divine spirit; so thankful that I have walked very close to the Lord.

A Christmas Spirit

This supernatural event happened in December 24, 2007 at the Church of God In Christ, my sister her daughter and myself went to a Christmas program at the church it was our 1ˢᵗ visit at the new location, since it was going to be a crowd I decided that we should leave early to get a jump of seats and a good parking place up close. Well everything was going as plan we found good parking and was heading up the steps to the sanctuary when we noticed this homeless woman standing on the steps, as we passed her she held her hand out and asked for a quarter, my sister wanted to stop and give her some money. As she was digging in her purse for change, I said to my sister "don't worry about her we will give you something on our way out of service". We kept walking; my sister did not feel comfortable with my sarcastic remark to the homeless woman, so I turned to the homeless woman and said "I will give you some money on our way out of service". She smiled; we proceed into the sanctuary to find our seats. As we sat down my sister noticed the homeless woman was three rows ahead of us she said "Isn't that the homeless lady that was outside of the church" as I was trying to get into the service all we could see was the back of her head. I said to my sister "I don't think so" she is probable still outside begging for money. Then my sister was dissatisfied with my answer, then firmly she said "look again Linda" I know that is that lady, cause I recognize the hat she was wearing. When I finally took a second look at her I notice that it was her, we looked at each other with amazement, and about that time the homeless lady turned around

and smiled me I remembered that smile from outside at the steps. I said "how did she get in the church before we did", my sister started to get upset with me and said "I told you we should have given that lady some money, now look what you did with your big mouth", I told my sister "don't worry" I will fix this and give her some money now. As I began digging in my purse for some change, suddenly the homeless lady rose up out of her seat, started heading towards the exit. I hurried and pulled out a dollar and as she passed us I had barely exited my seat, now I following a few feet behind her in the aisle row, and I started heading towards the exit. I was moving fast to catch up with her, she was moving like she was on an escalator. She was at least 2' ft in front of me I wasn't able to catch up with her, it seem as if I wasn't going to catch her before she got outside the building. I started screaming from the top of my voice as loud as I could, "lady please stop, please" but she just kept on going. The congregation was all entering the building as they were being ushered to their seats. It was very strange that no one noticed me screaming or running in the church there was no one observing my actions. It wasn't until she was outside the church at the steps the same position that we first met her when we were arriving to the sanctuary, she landed in the exact same location. Ultimately she stopped and looked at me, with panic in my voice and almost out of breath from chasing her I said "I am so sorry, please forgive me" at that moment I said to her "I don't have a quarter, but I have a dollar to give you, "she just smiled" it was the strangest smile I have ever seen in my life. Her teeth were yellow as if she had been homeless for a while; her skin was dry and dirty. As I went back inside the church, said told my sister "I caught up with her and gave her a dollar" the Christmas service began, it was an Angel of God that was disguised as a homeless woman, looked over at my sister and said "Let's enjoy the Christmas program".

As the Christmas service started, the Bishop was up speaking when he had this interruption that came with a loud voice saying "Alleluia" and it was a deep male voice that kept say "Alleluia" as *everyone was looking around to see who was saying this. I turned around behind me and there he was Michael the Archangel he put out his hand for me to shake it, and I did shake his hand. The power of the Lord was all over me, I was gone in the Spirit. About that time I heard the Bishop telling the entire congregation to stand to their feet, and start Praising God. He said "We have the Spirit of the Lord in the house". When I heard him say that I never looked up again until service was over, and I praised the Lord throughout the entire service. It was the best service I have ever attended, my sister received her healing of her asthma, and she said "I felt a warm hand on my back". My plan is to visit Church of God In Christ again soon.*

Vision of 911

Incidents the Lord Jesus had given me a vision about 2-3 weeks prior to the collision of the Twin Towers, and I was having a vision of the collision people running for their lives in a mass of confusion. I was standing across the street when all of a sudden there was a gulf of fire explosion. I looked up and there was the building in a collapse stage and the second aircraft was flying towards the second Tower and I saw people running for their lives and the flames were enormous. Then I was awakened. This was continuous until about 2 weeks before the actual destruction of the Twin Towers and I was devastated. While I was having this vision I would broadcast the dream to everyone that I would encounter with my job, my church, my friends, even strangers. I would say "there is going to be a disaster and a lot of people are going to lose their life, we need to pray to change the course of the event". Some people thought I was crazy and some would catch me privately and ask questions about the vision. But people thought if it be anything it was an earthquake, and I would broadcast this for months, until about 2 weeks prior and I would pray like it was no tomorrow. On the morning of September 11, 2001 I was on my way to work, when over the radio the announcement came in as the first aircraft had flown into the Twin Tower that was only the first Tower involved, I said to myself as I was on the highway, "My God help us". Then as I continued going into the work area all my co-workers were standing around the radio, and the room was quite no one was speaking, as I went to my desk to get started they walked over to

me and said have you heard? I said "heard what". That a Boeing aircraft flew into the Twin Tower about that time the second aircraft hit the second Tower and I started screaming, and crying I said all those people buried and the lives lost, and I was crying loud, so they tried to calm me down, and I just lost it and wanted to go home, but my co-workers felt I should stay because I was not showing any stability. They said we don't feel you should be at home by yourself, as they continued watching the news reports I was still screaming "all those innocent lives buried". Then the guys start to say they haven't give out that information yet, we don't know if anyone has gotten hurt. I screamed loud of numbers so larger that it frighten everyone in the room. I said over thousands of people dead and I would cry so hard and the pain I was feeling that day was just too much to bear.

Now my co-workers separated me into one of the offices to calm down, and it was horrible all I could see was the lives that had been lost. When the third plane crashed I wasn't in the room with the rest of the co-workers and they were not about to tell me anything because I was completely out of control. When I finally left work around 2pm I rushed to the news channel and sat there with unbelief, I was so disgusted that I went to church that evening crying all the way, talking to the Lord the entire time I couldn't understand why would this happen and no one would believe me. When I pulled up into the church parking lot people came towards my car, when I got out they were asking "Sister Linda did you hear what happened"? I said "yes, I did". Then they asked me is there anything God is telling you now; I said "No" went inside the church and prayed for everyone in New York, and all the families involved. Then I went home and God was working on me, I was told to send a letter, and so I began to write the letter. When I got to work I typed the letter out and sent it to the Vice-President of the Boeing Company, and he was impressed and held a meeting, and showed my letter to the staff. I was embarrassed because I had never done anything like this before, so the letter eventually made its way to the United States President. I still have the documentations of the written letter and the type written letter. I believe that if more people would have believed me and we would have joined into prayer things could have turned out different. I was given the insight of how the United States will be affected in the future behind the incident, and every report I gave was not a good report and the Famine that we are experiencing now would have been deviated but my warning was too late because of unbelief. Many people are suffering today.

Epilogue

This book will complete you with knowledge and wisdom on how I was chosen to access God's Supernatural Power's and uses it for His Glory. To help reach a world that has lost touch with who God is and what is his purpose and plan for our lives. Everyone knows about the Holy Ghost Power that has been in the churches for years, but the power that Jesus mentioned comes from the Living God, "You will be able to do greater works than these". The power from the Living God is what people are searching for thru our Lord and Savior; we can only obtain it through the Holy Spirit. We actually have a generation who no longer believe that the Supernatural Powers of God can be more than what the bible speaks concerning things not seen. We have a responsibility to inform them of our God's Spiritual Power and we must excise in that power, follow the instructions that our Heavenly Father has laid before the foundations of the world and not deviate. Whenever I would hear with my spiritual ear it's opened, intended for reception of messages and conversations that God would allow me to hear, this was extraordinary. There have been times that I would repeat the conversations that I would hear to the person it was intended for and that would only spook the person, although I must admit I would have fun with the response I would get from that person. But most of all they would get further away from me, making it seem like I have a problem.

The Supernatural Power is awesome. It gets you right at the entry gate, into areas of life that no man on earth came close. Only thru

Jesus Christ who has the key that opened the door, and when he trust you enough to receive it you must follow instructions. There comes with a list of dos and don'ts included. If I wouldn't had follow the instructions that Jesus gave to me, I wouldn't ever been able to reach a level of his Supernatural Power's. The Holy Ghost is to guide us through all situations and problems, and empower us with what is needed to defeat the enemy. Since God has empowered me to call things as they are, not should be, because in the Supernatural God is always working in the Now. Today the empowerment of the Supernatural is greatly needed in society, so the world can be around from generation to generations; our children can enjoy the benefits of a world that God created through Love. It occurred to me that anyone of the saints has the power to operate in Faith, let us try the Now Faith and move into the operation of God's Supernatural Power and change the world today.

I don't believe that God is ready to destroy the world yet; he wants to clean it up, and have the next generation's lives be not destroyed but the present people of God. To continue reaching higher levels in God's Supernatural Power's, just like when Abraham asked God to spare Sodom and Gomorrah, if enough of God's people would reach a higher level in him it could have been done. People of God with your Faith you can change God's mind about a situations or circumstances. It fascinates me when people of God can read the scriptures and not be able to perform the miracles that Jesus was able to perform. I believe they are still waiting for the Messiah to come down from Heaven and zap them with power to go into the world, somewhat like super hero's does in the movies. The power is already within you waiting to be utilized by the people of God, and you have already been given authority to access his Supernatural Powers you just need God's operational instructions.

Now is the time to make it happen, we are in a crisis more so than ever in life. I don't know why, when people receive the Holy Ghost they limit the power to this world only, when you can do so much more through Faith in the Living God. When it comes to the Supernatural Powers people really don't believe in the existence of the next level or like I said fear takes control, or just want the goodies houses, money and cars. People of God, it is time to deviate from just capitalization of material things it life, because those things will not have any value when life ends. Place some of your Faith in the Supernatural Power's of God which has dominion over the future, past and present.

There's really no comparison to the Supernatural Power's preceding what heights that God has placed within our spirit, but we choose the things of this world because of the limitation of the knowledge and understanding the Most High God. When you tell people that you can reach into the atmosphere of another world they only want to call you crazy, psycho or just plain weird.

About the Author

Since early childhood, I was always passionate about writing, born in Los Angeles, California. Participation in drama, my first play was written at the age of 15 while attending J.F. Kennedy H.S. in Granada Hills.

Begin working my way through Hollywood applying for employment, as a Secretary since I did have skills. Started working at Capitol Records then transferred to ABC Records, I wanted to further my education with classes in production attended American Broadcasting School and Columbia Broadcasting School in Hollywood. Then I relocated to Florida where I begin working on my career at a small radio station, giving the time of day, and then transferred to the newspaper company Sentinel Star. Relocated to Washington State began working at The Boeing Company.

Printed in the United States
By Bookmasters